Beginning
Mandolin

by Bob Grant

Amsco Publications
New York/London/Sydney

Cover photograph of Gibson F5 by Randall Wallace
Project editor: Ed Lozano
Interior design and layout: Don Giller

Order No. AM 941369
US International Standard Book Number: 0.8256.1574.7
UK International Standard Book Number: 0.7119.6170.0

Exclusive Distributors:
Music Sales Corporation
257 Park Avenue South, New York, NY 10010 USA
Music Sales Limited
8/9 Frith Street, London W1V 5TZ England
Music Sales Pty. Limited
120 Rothschild Street, Rosebery, Sydney, NSW 2018, Australia

Printed in the United States of America by
Vicks Lithograph and Printing Corporation

Contents

To Tracie,
who always keeps me pointed in the right direction.

Preface

Like many mandolinists, I discovered the mandolin after being a guitar player for a number of years. The first time I came across a mandolin was while playing guitar in a theater production. The bass player in the group started bringing a mandolin to the theater to kill time in between shows. I had never seen one up close or heard one live before, but I instantly fell in love with it. The owner of the mandolin would often leave it unattended in the backstage area. I would pick it up and noodle around on it. I figured out a few chords after finding out how to tune it. . . I was hooked. The mandolin was it. I found myself playing every chance I had. When the show ended, my days of playing mandolin ended also. But as luck would have it, a few months later a friend of a friend was selling a frying-pan mandolin that his father had given him as a gift. He needed the money quick, so I ended up getting a good deal on a decent mandolin of my own. Now that I had my own mandolin, I found myself playing it more and more and playing the guitar less and less.

I had no idea what kind of music was played on the mandolin or even who played one. The only people I had ever seen or heard playing the mandolin were Jimmy Page (from Led Zeppelin) and Peter Buck (of R.E.M.). I soon found out, however, that the mandolin is a lot more common that I thought. The mandolin is used in folk, country, blues, Italian, Irish, Klezmer, and bluegrass music. There are even concertos by Vivaldi and Mozart written for mandolin. I love all these kinds of music, but bluegrass is what really got me excited about playing mandolin.

It is hard to imagine where the mandolin would be today if it were not for Bill Monroe and his bluegrass music. In the early 1900s, the mandolin was in its heyday. There were mandolin orchestras and mandolin clubs all across the country. By the 1920s, the mandolin's popularity was superseded by the banjo, which was in turn eclipsed by the guitar in the 1930s. When Bill was young, the mandolin was thought of as a child's instrument. But in Monroe's hands, the mandolin proved to be a versatile and worthy opponent to the banjo, guitar, and fiddle, capable of creating a soft delicate tremolo or a blazing hot solo. Bluegrass is where the mandolin has thrived. Just go to any bluegrass festival and you will see more mandolins than you thought you would see in your whole life.

No matter what kind of music turns you on, you are bound to find the mandolin in there somewhere.

Strings and Fingers

You have bought your first mandolin. If it is new, it will probably have new strings on it. If it is a used mandolin, chances are that the strings are pretty worn and a new set would be a good idea. Your local music store can put a new set on for you. Not only will new strings sound better but if you've never played a stringed instrument before, they might be a little easier on your fingers. Playing the mandolin as with any stringed instrument, involves a little bit of getting your finger tips accustomed to pressing down strings. It will make your fingers sore for a short period of time until you develop calluses.

Practicing

Practice every day, even if you can only squeeze in a few minutes a day. It will be better than a couple of hours once or twice a week. You will retain more of what you learn. At home I keep my mandolin in a place that I walk by often. Everytime I go past it, I pick it up and play for a while. Instead of slaving over the instrument for hours on end, I have a great time playing for shorter periods of time *all day*. My practice time is usually spent playing along with recordings, playing rhythm as well as the melodies. Everyone has a different approach to practicing. The main thing I have found is to remember to have fun, and if you start to become bored, put it down and come back to it later.

Holding the Mandolin

Always use a strap. Having played the mandolin for many years, I still find it uncomfortable to play without a strap, even while sitting down. Using a strap holds the mandolin in a way that lets your hands move more freely. A narrow strip of leather or cord wrapped around the headstock between the tuners and the nut and the other end fastened to the end pin works well.

The Pick

Choosing the right kind of pick and the way you hold it determines how your mandolin will sound. This is your volume and tone control. Picks come in all shapes and sizes as well as degrees of stiffness. I generally use the hardest picks that I can find because they are louder and have a thicker tone. However, they can be a little hard to control at first so you might want to start with a medium pick until you get the hang of it. I think the bigger full size picks (Fender heavy shapes) are the best because there is more surface area and more to hold on to so you will not drop them.

The way that you hold the pick is very important. After a lot of trial and error, I found the correct way to hold a pick and when I finally did, my playing got better immediately. I had better tone, could play with more power, more volume and still remained relaxed.

Relax your right hand. Make an open fist keeping your thumb straight and resting it on your first knuckle of your index finger. Place the pick between you index finger and thumb, leaving the tip of your thumb extending over the edge of the pick a little bit. This might feel a bit awkward at first but stick with it and you will find your reward will be control, volume, and tone.

Tuning

Mitch Jayne of the Dillards once said that tuning a mandolin is like tuning a set of bedsprings. Tuning can be tricky, but like anything else, if you know the procedure it should get easier with practice. The mandolin, as you may have noticed, has eight strings. It helps to think of it as four sets of two strings with each set tuned to the same note. The mandolin is played as if it has only four strings.

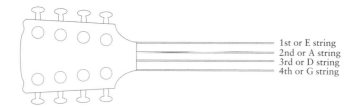

1st or E string
2nd or A string
3rd or D string
4th or G string

Tuning to the Piano

Tuning your mandolin to a piano is as simple as it gets. Simply tune the G strings (the two strings closest to your head) to the G note below middle C on the piano by turning the corresponding tuners at the headstock until they match the pitch on the piano. Tune the D strings to the D note above middle C on the piano and the A strings to the A above middle C. And finally, tune the E strings to the second E above middle C. Repeat the process once or twice to fine tune the instrument.

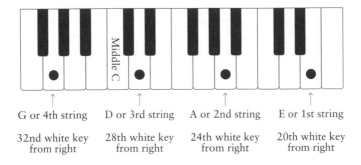

↑	↑	↑	↑
G or 4th string	D or 3rd string	A or 2nd string	E or 1st string
32nd white key from right	28th white key from right	24th white key from right	20th white key from right

The Tuning Fork

Tuning your mandolin to a tuning fork is a little more involved than tuning to a piano. It is more convenient however, as a piano is a little harder to carry around.

Finding a tuning fork is fairly easy. Most music stores carry them. I have always used an A tuning fork because they seem to be the most common.

First, tap the fork on any hard surface (a table, wall, your knee, etc.) and touch the handle to the bridge of the mandolin. The pitch you hear is an A note. Tune the A strings (the second pair of strings from the floor) to the A note. Your A strings are now in tune and you can tune the rest of your strings to them. This can be done by pressing the D (third) strings down at the seventh fret and matching those notes to the open A (second) strings. Now tune the G (fourth) strings the same way: Press the G strings at the seventh fret and match them to the open D strings. Finally, tune the E (first) strings by fretting the A strings at the seventh fret and matching the open E strings to the fretted A strings. I usually repeat these steps a few times because as the tension on the strings is changed, the neck and top of the mandolin will give and take.

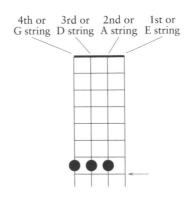

4th or G string   3rd or D string   2nd or A string   1st or E string

These same steps can be used to tune your mandolin from a guitar or any other instrument that is in tune. All you need is a G, D, A, or E note and you can tune all your strings from that note.

Electronic Tuners

Electronic tuners can be very helpful when you are first learning. While you should know how to tune without an electronic tuner, it does help you get right down to the business of learning how to play a little bit sooner. Most tuners are very simple to use and can be plugged in or used with a built-in microphone. Almost all have a needle and/or LEDs, and using one is just a matter of tuning the string until the needle is in the middle of the meter. They all have little differences, so read the instructions.

Chord Diagrams

Let's get down to business. First we will look at a chord diagram. This is basically a picture of the fretboard as if you were holding the mandolin in front of you with the headstock pointed upwards. The heavy line across the top is the nut and the lighter horizontal lines beneath it are the frets. The four vertical lines are the strings. Although the mandolin has eight strings, it helps to think of it as having only four since they are doubled.

Reading the chord diagram is very simple. The dots show you at which frets to press down the strings and what fingering to use. For example, the diagram below has a dot with the number 2 in it on the first string at the third fret. The dot represents the tip of your second finger pressing the first string down at the third fret. The fingers of the left hand are numbered 1 through 4. 1 is the index, 2 the middle, 3 the ring finger, and 4 the pinky. So in this example, we are using the middle finger.

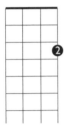

Chords

A *chord* is a grouping of two or more notes played at the same time. I am sure you have seen a guitar player strumming an acoustic guitar. He or she was hitting all the strings of the guitar at the same time. Those were chords. Chords are fuller sounding than single notes and are used to back up the melody of a song either sung by a vocalist or played by another instrument. The two types of chords we will look at are major and minor.

Now on to our first major chords. Let's begin with a G chord.

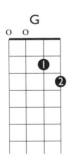

Once the fingers of your left hand are in place, brush the pick across all the strings at the same time. This is called *strumming* the chord. If the chord does not sound clear or any note is buzzing, check your left-hand fingering. Try again, making sure that when you *fret* a note (press a string down) you are pressing right behind the fret, almost on top of it. The zeros above the third and fourth strings mean that those strings are *open*. In other words, they are played but not fretted.

Now let's look at a D chord:

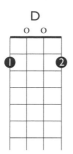

After your left hand is in position, strum the chord. Be sure to let the two open middle strings ring freely. The key to getting a good clean chord is making sure you use the very tips of your fingers and not the fleshy pads. You might also want to make sure that your fingernails are fairly short. Long fingernails will prevent you from being able to press the string down firmly against the fingerboard and result in poor tone or buzzing strings.

Now let's try a C chord.

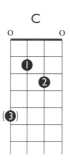

You will notice that the *3* is in parentheses, this only means that the chord can be played with or without that note fretted. If you do not fret that note, play the open string. The only difference is that the chord sounds a little stronger with the third finger added. You might find the stretch between your second and third fingers a little uncomfortable at first–but don't worry, your hand will become used to it.

You now know three chords, and while this does not seem like much, thousands of songs are now virtually at your fingertips. Many folk, bluegrass, and rock songs require no more than these three chords.

In the following exercise, the name of the chord that is to be played is shown above the *staff* (the five horizontal lines). The light vertical lines are called *barlines*. The space between the barlines is called a *bar* or *measure*. Each measure has four *beats*. The dark slashes in the middle of the staff represent strums of the chord. In this case, four strums would be played for each chord, one strum for each beat. When practicing, make sure that you keep a steady, even tempo. It's not how fast you play, but how smoothly you can change from one chord to another. The speed will come with practice.

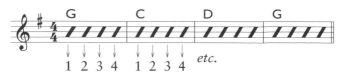

Since we just learned three chords in the key of G, let's try the old folk song "Jesse James." "Jesse James" has been a favorite of bluegrass musicians since the late fifties, when it was recorded by the Country Gentlemen on their first album. So if you go to a festival and play in a jam session, the chances are that everyone will know it. We are just going to play the chords right now. We will go back and look at the melody later. Remember to keep the rhythm smooth and steady and try to play the chords as clearly as possible. Try counting aloud to help you get the feel of four beats per measure.

Jesse James

Poor Jesse had a wife to mourn for his life,
Three children they were brave,
But the dirty little coward that shot Mr. Howard,
Has laid Jesse James in his grave.

It was Robert Ford, that dirty little coward,
I wonder how he does feel,
For he ate of Jesse's bread and he slept in Jesse's bed,
Then he laid poor Jesse in his grave.

Jesse James was a man, a friend to the poor,
He'd never see a man suffer pain;
And with his brother Frank, he robbed the Chicago
    bank,
And stopped the Glendale train.

It was on a Wednesday night and the moon was shining
    bright,
They robbed the Glendale train,
And the people they did say for many miles away,
It was robbed by Frank and Jesse James.

It was his brother Frank that robbed the Gallatin bank,
And carried the money from town;
It was in this very place that they had a little race,
For they shot Captain Sheets to the ground.

They went to the crossing not very far from there,
And there they did the same;
With the agent on his knees, he delivered up the keys
To the outlaws, Frank and Jesse James

It was on a Saturday night and Jesse was home
Talking with his family brave,
Robert Ford came along like a thief in the night
And laid poor Jesse in his grave.

The people held their breath when they heard of Jesse's
    death
And wondered how he ever came to die.
It was one of the gang called little Robert Ford,
He shot poor Jesse on the sly.

Jesse went to rest with his hand on his breast,
The devil would be upon his knee.
He was born one day in the county of Clay,
And came from a solitary race.

This song was made by Billy Gashade
As soon as the news did arrive;
He said there was no man with the law in his hand
Who could take Jesse James when alive.

It's important not to over-think this stuff. Some of our biggest holes we have to climb out of, we dig ourselves. All the things we have been talking about until now simply tell you to put your left-hand fingers where the dots are and strum the chord once for each tap of your foot in a steady rhythm.

With a little practice, you will find that your hand will be able to snap right into the correct chord shape without thinking about it. This is called *muscle memory*. It's kind of like working the remote control for the television, after a while your fingers just seem to know where to go without your really thinking about it.

Now onward to more chords. Let's take a shot at an F chord. Remember that you do not have to press the strings down very hard if you press right behind the frets.

Now that you know an F chord, we can try a tune in the key of C that uses the C, F, and G chords. "Will the Circle Be Unbroken" is a traditional song that has been recorded many times since the Carter family first did it in the late twenties. The most popular version that I know of is the Nitty Gritty Dirt Band's version on the album of the same name. It is also very popular among folk and bluegrass musicians and is bound to pop up at many jam sessions.

Will the Circle Be Unbroken

I was standing by the window
On one cold and cloudy day;
And I saw the hearse come rolling
For to carry my mother away.

Lord, I told the undertaker,
"Undertaker, please drive slow;
For this body you are hauling,
Lord, I hate to see her go."

I followed close behind her,
Tried to hold up and be brave;
But I could not hide my sorrow
When they laid her in the grave.

Went back home, Lord, my home was lonesome
Since my mother she was gone:
All my brothers, sisters crying,
What a home so sad and lone.

Until now we have been using a straight right-hand rhythm only on the beats (1-2-3-4). Now we are going to try strumming some different rhythm patterns. The following example shows a standard eighth-note pattern.

When playing this exercise, it is very important to tap your foot. First just try counting without playing so you can get your foot moving in the right direction. Count 1-2-3-4 when your foot is down and the &s when your foot is up. Be sure to keep a steady rhythm.

All the strums should be played downward. Try to play just the two lowest strings of the chord on the beat and the whole chord on the offbeat. Be sure to let the notes ring out. This will make the strumming sound smoother. It will seem awkward at first because your foot is going up and down while your hand is only going down, but with practice this will feel very natural. Try this rhythm on both of the songs that you have already learned.

The next two chords are going to be an A chord and an E chord. These are a little different from the other chords because they don't have open strings.

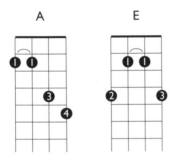

Each of these chords require you to use one finger to press two strings down at the same time. This is called a *bar chord*. When I was first learning to play, I found bar chords very difficult. I just could not get all the notes to come out clearly. I found that the key to this was *not* to mash your fingers down so hard, but to *relax your hand and apply even pressure across all of the strings*. These chords take a little more practice than the others because it may take a while for your hands to build up the strength to play them easily.

"The Banks of the Ohio" is an old type of folk song called a *murder ballad*. There are many murder ballads in folk, bluegrass, and blues music. They are story songs that tell primarily of love and jealousy. Many performers have recorded this song, but my favorite version is by Bill Monroe and Doc Watson. Their rendition is sung as a duet with only a mandolin and guitar accompaniment.

The Banks of the Ohio

Moderately slow

I asked my love to take a walk,
Just a lit - tle way with me.
And as we walked a-long we talked
All a - bout our wed-ding day.

Then only say that you'll be mine,
In no other arms entwine.
Down beside where the waters flow,
On the banks of the Ohio.

I asked your mother for you, dear,
And she said you were too young;
Only say that you'll be mine—
Happiness in my home you'll find.

I held a knife against her breast,
And gently in my arms she pressed,
Crying: Willie, oh Willie, don't murder me,
For I'm unprepared for eternity.

I took her lily white hand,
Led her down where the waters stand.
I picked her up and I pitched her in,
Watched her as she floated down.

I started back home 'twixt twelve and one,
Crying, My God, what have I done?
I've murdered the only woman I love,
Because she would not be my bride.

You might notice that the A and E chor.
really just the G chord and the D chord shapes
moved up two frets and playing what would be the
open strings with a bar. These chords are therefore
moveable. This means that by moving them up
and down the neck, you can play different chords
but still use the same chord shape.

Play an A chord and then move the A chord
two frets up, now it is B chord.

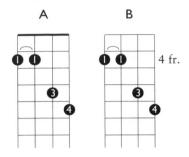

If you move that chord shape up one fret more
it becomes a C chord. That is how moveable
chords work: you only need to know a few chord
shapes and you can play almost any chord.

"The East Virginia Blues" is a song that I
learned from a recording by Keith Whitley when
he used to play with a band called the Country
Store. Many artists have recorded this tune,
including the Stanley Brothers and the Kentucky
Colonels. This one will give you a chance to
practice the B chord. We'll play it in the key of E.

18

The East Virginia Blues

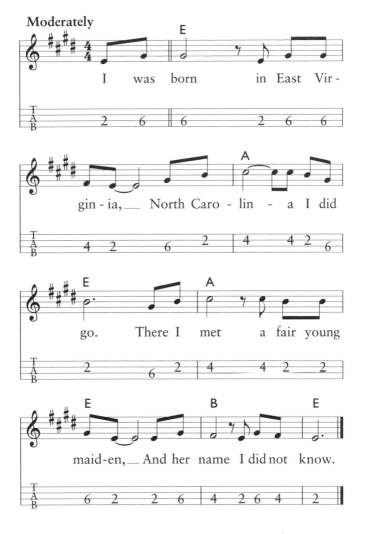

Moderately

I was born in East Vir-
gin-ia,___ North Caro-lin-a I did
go. There I met a fair young
maid-en,___ And her name I did not know.

Well, her hair was dark in color
And her cheeks were rosy red;
On her breast she wore white lilies
Where I long to lay my head.

I'd rather be in some dark holler,
Where the sun refuses to shine,
Than for you to be another man's darling,
And to know you'll never be mine.

Another variation of the right-hand rhythm
you might want to try the one that uses *upstrokes*.
Make a G chord and play this familiar rhythm

1 & 2 & 3 & 4 &

Now add an upstroke on each *a*.

1 & a 2 & a 3 & a 4 & a

This rhythm sounds like a horse galloping or a
"boom chicka boom chicka." Your right hand
should play downstrokes on the *1 &* and one
upstroke on the *a*. Once again, it is important to
keep your foot tapping.

Minor Chords

Up until now we have only been using major
chords. Now we are going to look at *minor
chords*. Minor chords have a very different sound
from major chords. Minor chords have a sadder or
darker sound. I usually think of them as having a
Middle Eastern flavor.

There are two useful minor chord shapes that
you should know. The first in an A minor chord.
The *root* (the note that the chord is named after) is
on the G string. The only difference between the
minor and the major chord shape is that the note
played on the A string is *flatted* (lowered) one fret.

Am

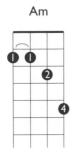

I learned "Omie Wise" from a recording of
Doc Watson at the Newport Folk Festival in 1963.
It has also been recorded by Joan Baez as well as
Bob Dylan. "Omie Wise" not only uses an A
minor chord but it is also in the key of A minor,
which gives the song a very lonesome, melancholy
sound.

Omie Wise

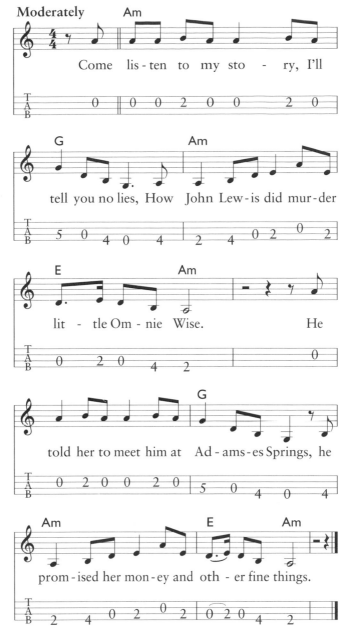

He gave her no money, but flattered the case,
Saying, "We will get married, 'twill be no disgrace."

She got up behind him, away they did go,
Down to the river where the fast waters flow.

"John Lewis, John Lewis, please tell me your mind,
Do you mean to marry me or leave me behind?"

"Little Omie, Little Omie, I'll tell you my mind,
My mind is to drown you and leave you behind."

He beat her and banged her 'til she could hardly go,
Then he threw her in the river where the fast waters
    flow.

Two little boys went fishing just at the break of dawn,
They saw little Omie come floating along.

They arrested John Lewis, they arrested him today,
They buried little Omie down in the cold clay.

"My name is John Lewis, my name I'll never deny,
I murdered little Omie, now I'm condemned to die."

"Go hang me, go kill me, for I am the man,
who murdered little Omie down by the mill dam."

Remember that you can use any of the right-hand rhythms that you have learned so far. When you feel comfortable with them, try mixing them up. One combination that I often use is a "boom chick boom chicka."

The root for the E minor chord in the following example is on the D string. This chord shape is the same as the E major except the note played on the E string is lowered one fret. Both the Em and Am chord shapes are moveable.

Em

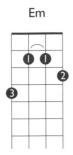

"Sitting on Top of the World" is a very popular traditional song that has been played in almost all genres of music. It is particularly popular with blues and folk artists. It has also been known to pop up at Grateful Dead concerts every now and then.

"Sitting on Top of the World" uses a minor chord, but it is not in a minor key.

Sitting on Top of the World

Bluegrass Chords

There is a certain way of playing chords on a mandolin in bluegrass that is different from other kinds of music. Bluegrass mandolinists play chords using fingerings different from the ones we have looked at. One of the reasons for this is that Bill Monroe, the "Father of Bluegrass," played them like this. And who am I to question the Big Mon? The technical reason stems from the fact that the traditional bluegrass band does not have drums. Playing chords this way makes them more percussive, so they sound almost like a snare drum. These chords are moveable so you can use the same shapes in any key.

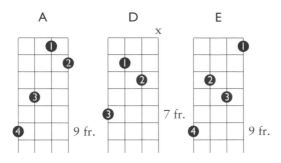

Up until now all the right-hand rhythms that we have learned have been very guitar oriented. These rhythms do not work well in bluegrass. The classic right-hand rhythm in bluegrass is called a *chop*. A chop is a short, sharp strum played on every offbeat. To play a chop, you have to strum the chord with your right hand and immediately release it with your left hand. It is almost as if the strum and release happen at the same time. A good chop is the driving force in a bluegrass band, but it is not easy and requires a lot of practice.

Single String Study

Tablature

It is now time to go back and play the melodies to the songs that you have played as chord arrangements. First, you need to know how to read *tablature (TAB)*. Tablature is a music notation shorthand for stringed instruments which is very easy to read. All you need to know is that the four horizontal lines represent the four double strings of the mandolin, and how to read the rhythm notation. The numbers tell you where to fret the strings and the stems connected to the noteheads in the standard music notation tell you the duration of the notes. It is similar to reading the chord diagrams.

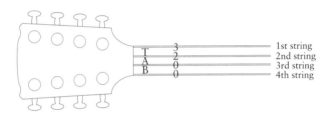

Reading rhythm notation is pretty simple. Look at the beginning of a song and you will see the *time signature* or *meter marking*. The number on top tells the number of beats per measure and the bottom number says what type of note gets one beat. A $\frac{4}{4}$ time signature says that there are four beats per measure and that a quarter note gets one beat. This is the most common meter in music.

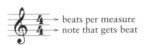

There are five *rhythmic values* (kinds of notes) that you need to know. Whole notes, half notes, quarter notes, eighth notes, and sixteenth notes. In $\frac{4}{4}$ time, a *quarter note* gets one beat, a *whole note* gets four beats, and a *half note* gets two beats. There are two *eighth notes* to a beat and four *sixteenth notes* to a beat.

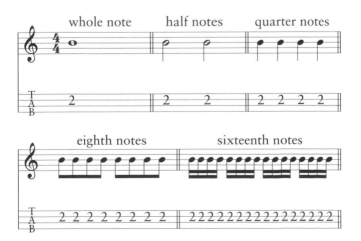

A *note* is identified by the stem that is attached to the notehead.

 eighth note    sixteenth note

If there are two of more notes smaller than a quarter note played consecutively, they may be beamed together.

Eighth notes are counted like this.

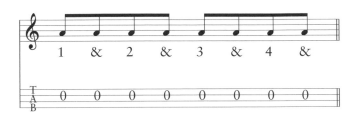

Sixteenth notes are counted like this.

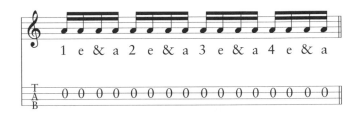

A *dot* following a note tells you to add half the value of that note to the basic note value. For example, a *dotted quarter note* would get one and a half beats. A *dotted half note* would get three beats and so on.

Sometimes a melody requires that there be a pause. *Rests* are the places in a melody that you do not play (you rest). There is a rest symbol equal in value to every note. When you see a rest, stop playing but keep counting.

Try playing the melody to "The Banks of the Ohio" (page 17). Notice that in every other measure there is a whole note with three dark slanted lines below it, this is a tremolo marking. *Tremolo* is the rapid repetition of a note using upstrokes and downstrokes. Since the mandolin is an instrument of limited sustain, tremolo is sometimes used to hold a note for its full value. In this case, the whole-note tremolo lasts for four beats.

When playing tremolo be sure to keep tapping your foot. Do not tense up your arm because this will make the tremolo sound choppy. If you relax your arm, your tremolo will sound smoother, and you will have more endurance.

Now we will try the minor melody to "Omie Wise" (page 21). There are two things about this melody that might be a little difficult. The first is the dotted quarter notes. A dotted-quarter-note followed by an eighth note creates *syncopation*. The second hard part is the dotted-eighth-note rhythm which sounds exactly the same as the dotted-quarter-note rhythm played twice as fast. Practice this very slowly and keep counting while you hold the dotted notes. These measures are counted 1 a 2 & 3. There are a lot of eighth notes in this melody but you will find that the difficult parts are the ones that I just mentioned.

"Soldier's Joy" was the first instrumental tune that I learned when I started on the mandolin. It is a standard old-time tune that dates back to the Civil War. When the time comes for your first jam session, you can play this tune and everyone will probably know it.

It looks harder than it really is because there are quite a few notes. You will find, however, that the notes are mainly eighth notes in a consistent rhythm that is not too difficult. Play it slowly at first and gradually work it up to speed. The only tricky places are the dotted-eighth-notes.

Soldiers Joy

All of these things that you have learned should put you on the right track to playing the mandolin. This basic knowledge should get you through the first few months of playing. When you feel comfortable with this stuff (or even just a little comfortable!) go out and find a jam session so that you see and hear other mandolinists. I would recommend looking for a bluegrass, old-time, or Irish session in your area. All levels of players usually attend these informal gatherings, from beginners through advanced professionals. These sessions are great opportunities to learn in a no-pressure environment. The players like to meet new people showing interest in the music they love. Don't be afraid to ask questions, keep your eyes and ears open; watch and learn. Good luck and remember that the most important thing is to have fun.

Some great mandolinists that you might want to listen to are:

Bluegrass mandolinists **Bill Monroe, Frank Wakefield,** and **Sam Bush**
Klezmer/Bluegrass mandolinist **Andy Statman**
Dawg mandolinist **David Grisman**
Blues mandolinist **Yank Rachel**
Jazz mandolinists **Jethro Burns** and **Paul Glass**

Chord Dictionary

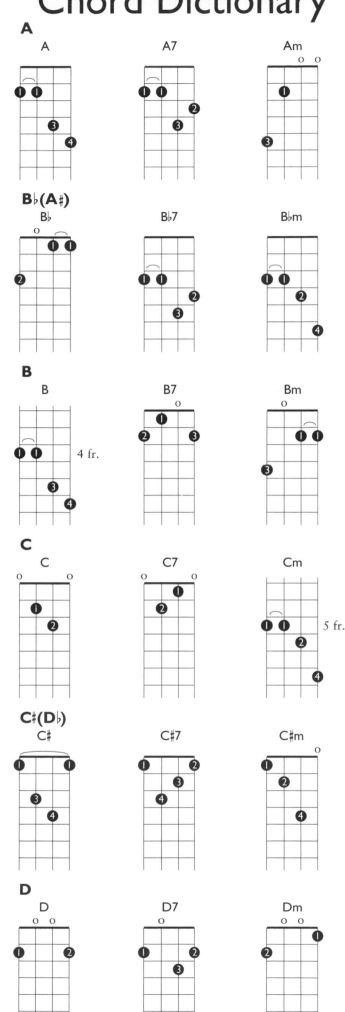

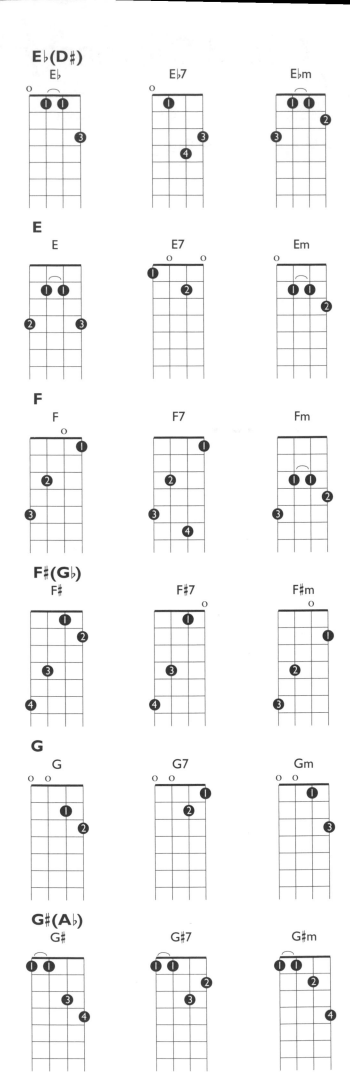

About the Author

Bob Grant is a member of the Austin-based trio the Bad Livers (who have recently signed a deal with Sugar Hill Records), and has also toured and recorded with Rounder recording artist Slaid Cleaves. He founded the Metropolitan Bluegrass Authority, an umbrella organization for bluegrass musicians, in New York City. When he's not touring with the Bad Livers, Bob lives in Manhattan where he plays with his band Drinkin' & Cheatin'. Bob is also a graduate of Boston's Berklee College of Music where he earned a B.F.A. in Film Score Composition; in addition, he is currently recording the soundtrack to the film, "The Newton Boys."